Academic Jokes

...Lighter side of Academics

S.M. Mathur

Published by:

V&S PUBLISHERS

F-2/16, Ansari Road, Daryaganj, New Delhi-110002
011-23240026, 011-23240027 • *Fax:* 011-23240028
Email: info@vspublishers.com • *Website:* www.vspublishers.com

Branch : Hyderabad
5-1-707/1, Brij Bhawan (Beside Central Bank of India Lane)
Bank Street, Koti, Hyderabad - 500 095.
040-24737290.
E-mail: vspublishershyd@gmail.com

Follow us on:

For any assistance sms **VSPUB** to **56161**
All books available at **www.vspublishers.com**

© Copyright: V&S Publishers
ISBN 978-93-813847-0-1
Edition 2013

The Copyright of this book, as well as all matter contained herein (including illustrations) rests with the Publishers. No person shall copy the name of the book, its title design, matter and illustrations in any form and in any language, totally or partially or in any distorted form. Anybody doing so shall face legal action and will be responsible for damages.

Printed at : Param Offseters, Okhla, New Delhi-110020

Humour gives relief from
Pain during any misfortune.

Abraham Lincoln said:
"I laugh because I must not cry"

From the Author's Desk.......

As we all know, making jokes is no joke, when particularly, it is on a subject like **Academics.** I have taken over two years to create and assemble these jokes and anecdotes.

I know we have a lot of people with a sense of humour and it would be that they would laugh when they read and re-read the jokes/anecdotes for which I had to energise my grey cells to meet the requirements of the readers.

A lot of the jokes in this book have been drawn from my personal experiences as well or have been created by me. So, keep smiling and remembering me, dear readers, as you read them, for nothing is as precious in the world as a smile on a face!

Contents

I	Academiscope	11
II	Examination Agony	38
III	School Capers	42
IV	Science Panorama	60
V	Geochronicle	66
VI	Cyber Symphony	69
VII	Bibliophile	78
VIII	Author! Author!	84
IX	The Queen's English	95
X	Medigogy	103

I

Academiscope

The Governor is the ex-officio Chancellor of the state universities. Many a time he is a politician with hardly any academic pretensions, but some try to show off. One such worthy Governor went for inspection to a university. As he entered the library, he saw before him a rack on which the latest arrivals were displayed—among which was a new edition of Shakespeare. "I am glad," remarked His Excellency, "that you have the latest works of Shakespeare. He is a great writer. I myself have enjoyed reading many of his novels. By the way, can you give me a list of his latest works?"

This anecdote was told at a function by Professor Hashim Ali, when he was the Vice-Chancellor of the Aligarh Muslim University.

Two men died and presented themselves before the pearly gates of heaven. St. Peter asked the first, "What were you doing when you were alive?"

"I was the Vice-Chancellor of an Indian university," said he.

"You have already suffered the torture of hell on earth and certainly deserve a place in Paradise."

The next person was asked the same question. "I was the Vice-Chancellor of an Indian university for three consecutive terms." he replied.

"Put him in Hell," ordered St. Peter. "He's got into the habit."

This brought the house down.

A politically-appointed Vice-Chancellor used to give himself a lot of airs. When a new edition of *Who's Who* came to the library, he was sure to find his name in it but it wasn't there.

"He should be in *Who's He?*" remarked a wag in the library.

Another Vice-Chancellor (V.C.) had the habit of saying, "Yes, you are right" to everyone, quite often contradicting himself. Not surprisingly, this caused utter confusion. One evening a group of students came demanding for the cancellation of a cricket match. He said: "You are right," and ordered cancellation. Moments later, when the cricket captain came to know about this, he rushed to the V.C. and protested: "This cannot be done as the other team has already reached here." Predictably, the V.C. said: "You are right."

The wife, who was a witness to this going-on, remarked in disgust: "You say, "You are right, to everyone."

"You are right, my dear," out came the pet reply and the wife left the place with utter disgust.

The post of Vice-Chancellor in a Bihar University was lying vacant for a long time as no one was prepared to risk his life. They required a strong man capable of taking on the rowdy students. So, it was seriously considered to invite some famous boxer to take on the job.

The Vice-Chancellors of several universities in North India have to face the onslaught of union and *netas,* particularly belonging to the ruling party in the state, and so have to think ways of protecting themselves. It is rumoured that a V.C. of a university in Bihar is contemplating to cover himself up in a suit of steel armour.

The participants at a seminar were thoroughly tired after three days of verbal outpourings by distended, self-important academics. At the valedictory function, the convener, himself, thoroughly exhausted, invited the chief guest. "I now request our revered Vice-Chancellor to give his address."

"Vice-Chancellor's Lodge, The University Campus," said the chief guest and sat down amidst thunderous applause.

In the early fifties of the last century, very few Indians could be seen on English streets, and a South Indian with his turban and all was indeed a rarity. One day, Professor Murthy, visiting the Eastern Philosophy Department at Oxford, was followed by a rowdy bunch of street urchins. He tolerated them for a while, but tired of their unwelcome attention, he turned around and shouted, "What do you want?"

"Coo," said one. "It speaks too."

It had been snowing in Quebec for hours when an announcement came on the intercom: "Will the students who have parked on the college drive, please move their cars so that we may start clearing the snow." Fifteen minutes later came another announcement: "Will the five hundred students who want to move the fifteen cars parked on the college drive return to their classes."

A moral science teacher was bemoaning the spread of promiscuity and AIDS.

At the end of the class, she asked, "Is there a virgin in this classroom? If there is, let her stand up." Nobody stood up for a while, and when she was about to resume, she noticed a young married student standing at the back with a baby in her arms.

"Excuse me young lady, did you understand the question? I asked if there was a virgin in the room?"

"Yes ma'am, said the mother, "but did you expect this three-month old baby to stand up by herself?"

The king of Greece came on a state visit to India in 1962. Welcoming him, President Sarvapalli Radhakrishnan said, "Your Majesty, you are the first King of Greece to come as our honoured guest. Alexander came uninvited."

In the good old days, when the Indians, who went for study in England, took a lot of taboos with themselves. They were particularly warned by their families about the enticing ways of English girls because at that time for an Indian to bring home an English bride was considered almost sacrilegious and merited ostracisation.

An Indian student ordered at a restaurant: "One coffee and vegetable sandwiches, please."

"Yes, with pleasure," acknowledged the pretty waitress.

"Oh, no." responded the student with alarm. "Only the food please, and no pleasure."

Attempts to ensure gender equality can sometimes have hilarious consequences. A university, trying to eliminate sexism from its adult education prospectus has offered a course in maternity and child care for 'pregnant persons'.

Gambling is a taboo in some cultures and is considered a sin. So, when the professor at the University of Reading, U.K., wanted to demonstrate a certain concept in statistics, he rolled a dice, but was not sure if the demonstration offended any foreign student in the class. He asked an Indian student: "Is this gambling demonstration offensive to you?"

"No," he replied. "But for gambling, there would not have been the Hindu epic, *Mahabharata!*"

A discussion was going on in the staff club about the intellectual attainments of people from various regions of India. It was generally agreed that Bengalis are very brainy but why? The Bengali lecturer boasted that it was due to their fish diet. Though a vegetarian, his Brahmin friend thought that he would test this contention by eating some fish. The Bengali promised to get him fish if he paid him five hundred rupees. So, the Pandit ate a tiny bit of fish supplied by the Bengali. Thinking about the matter, a little later, the Brahmin colleague confronted the Bengali. "Say," he asked doubtfully, "I don't think that such a little bit of fish should cost so much."

"See," exulted the Bengali, "You eat just a little bit of fish and become immediately wise to understand that five hundred rupees is too exorbitant a cost for a little bit of fish. So, now you know what happens to your brain if you eat fish regularly!"

At the farewell function, the passing out class was asked to tell what this university meant. A student stood up and declared: "My sister and I owe a lot to this university. You see—our parents met here."

Ramesh had lent some money to his neighbour. The loan was not repaid for long and whenever reminded, the borrower denied that he had ever borrowed any money. Ramesh did not know what to do and decided to seek the advice of his colleague in the psychology department.

"How much was the money?" asked the psychology professor.

"Five hundred rupees."

'Then go to him and demand double the amount."

"But how will it help me?"

"Do as I tell you and you will see."

So Ramesh went to his neighbour and

demanded, "You had borrowed a thousand rupees from me and now I want it back."

Off guard, the borrower blurted out, "I had borrowed only five hundred and now you demand a thousand, you crook."

Later, Ramesh went to his friend and thanked him.

"See, how psychology works," chuckled the professor.

In those times, when pro-Hindi agitation had swamped the entire country, students of a South Indian physics professor in Delhi University won't let him teach in English, shouting, "Hindi. Hindi." Annoyed, one day, he stepped up to the desk of a boy, caught hold of his wrist and said, "First throw away your watch with its imported dial in English and then I will adopt Hindi."

There was no trouble thereafter.

This happened in the 18th century. Lord Sandwich taunted the author, John Wilkes, "You will die of the pox or the gallows." Wilkes shot back: "That will depend on whether I embrace your Lordship's mistress or your Lordship's principles."

The economics teacher practised true economy and was a real penny-pincher. He was complaining about the spendthrift habits of his wife to a colleague. "One day, she asks me for twenty rupees, the next day for fifty, and this morning, she wants a hundred. She is the limit."

"She certainly is. What does she do with all the money?"

"How should I know? I never give her any!"

The venerable professor of economics complained that his memory was beginning to fade.

"But surely you remember that you borrowed a thousand rupees from me a month back," reminds a colleague.

"Oh yes! It remains one of my most pleasant memories," was the reply.

Like many academicians, a professor was averse to any physical exertion. If he was not reading a book, he was watching TV. His worried wife persuaded him to see a doctor. The doctor advised him to get some exercise.

"But I watch golf on the television," was the man's defence.

"No, no. This is no exercise; you need more exercise," remonstrated the doctor.

So now, he watches football on the television.

The professor of economics was describing the distinction between the financial terms 'bear' and 'bull'. He asked one student: "If you made a lot of investment in stocks and the market crashed, what will you be a bear or a bull?"

The student replied promptly: "Actually, an ass!"

A man was standing on the corner of a street with a begging bowl, asking for alms.

One man accosted him: "You appear to be quite an educated man, so why are you begging? Why don't you find some productive work?"

"Yes, I am a professor, and have written a book on *A Hundred Ways to Make Money*. This is one way."

Harold Laski, the noted professor at the London School of Economics, was requested once by the BBC radio to give a talk. The producer said, "Professor, I am afraid we cannot pay you much. The fee will only be five guineas."

The absent-minded Laski said, "It's alright. You will have my cheque in the post tomorrow."

Professor Milkiat Singh was invited at Professor Pandey's house for dinner. It suddenly started raining heavily and there was no let up even at midnight. Since Mr. Singh's family was away and he was alone, Mr. Pandey suggested that Mr. Singh spend the night with them. To this, Mr. Singh readily agreed and Mrs. Pandey went to prepare the guest room. Meanwhile, Mr. Singh disappeared and was found returning, dripping wet with a bundle under his arm. "Why, what happened?" enquired Mr. Pandey.

"I thought," replied Mr. Singh, "that if I have to spend the night here, I may as well get my night dress from my home."

An Indian professor of physics settled in the United States for long, blue-pencilled a doctorate dissertation rather severely, correcting the language and expression. The candidate was not amused and remonstrated, "Sir, how could you find fault with my language—my mother tongue is English."

To this, the professor remarked: "Your mother tongue may be English, but my wife's tongue is English. Now, Tell me, have you got more control over your mother or your wife?"

Many people in literature and humanities departments of Indian universities believe that copying from one source is plagiarism but copying from several sources is research.

A professor was disgusted with students, who came to him with absurd questions. Finally, he had a big board put up on the wall behind his desk:
"IT IS BETTER TO REMAIN SILENT
AND BE THOUGHT A FOOL
THAN TO SPEAK
AND REMOVE ALL DOUBT."

Professor Igor Strovonsky of the Friendship University, Moscow, is a visiting fellow at an Indian University. A victim of Delhi belly, he has now a *mantra* for eating: "While travelling in India, the rule should be eat, drink and be wary."

This is a profound observation by Professor Harry Rudin: "If an organization carries the word 'united' in its name, it means it isn't united. Examples are: United Nations, United Arab Emirates, United Kingdom, United States and so on......"

An American visiting professor at the Osmania University, Hyderabad, was invited to dinner by the Dean. The next day when I met him, he had a woebegone countenance. When I asked him how he had enjoyed the Andhra cuisine, he mournfully quipped: "The trouble with Andhra food is that it burns at both ends."

Politicians in India, particularly in the South, are enamoured to add the title of 'Dr.' before their names though they may have no academic accomplishments. The university authorities are also always eager to please their political masters. One such recent holder of the degree of Doctor of Letters, *honoris causa* got a phone call: "Is Dr. Maranna at home?" His seven-year old son replied: "No, he is not, but he is not the kind of doctor that can do you any good."

Waiters in restaurants around the university campus are used to the eccentricity of their clients. A professor sat down for lunch and after a look at the menu pulled out a notebook and started scribbling. After half-an-hour, he looked up to find a waiter hovering around him. He shouted, "Waiter, my bill," and took out his wallet.

British actor Albert Finney received an honorary doctorate from the University of Sussex. When he called up his father to give the news, the parent's comment was: "Doctor of Letters? You haven't written us a bloody postcard in three months and call yourself a Doctor of Letters!"

An absent-minded professor, his head buried in a volume, ordered a pizza. The waiter asked: "Sir, do you want it cut into four or eight pieces?"

Without looking up the don murmured: "Four, for I cannot eat eight," and continued poring over his book.

Two venerable academicians returning from the Nagpur Science Congress were travelling in the same coupe. The one on the upper berth snored like a lion in distress and the other spent the night turning on his berth cursing. When morning came, the snorer got down, yawned and asked his companion, "Professor, did you have a sound sleep?"

"Well," retorted the victim bitterly, "I had the sound and you had the sleep."

Harvard University maintains a record of its graduates, but the data are often incomplete. A university official was showing a list of their Nepali alumni to that country's ambassador. One entry read: *Birendra Bir Bikram Shah Dev—occupation unknown.* The Nepali official exclaimed: "But that is our king!"

At the end of the class on women fertility, the lecturer asked: "Should women have children after 35?"

A participant after a little thought said: "I think not. Thirty-five children are enough."

A parent's lament whose three children are in college: "I am getting poorer by degrees."

It was love at first sight. After a whirl-wind courtship, the professor from Delhi married the lovely dame from Mumbai attending the seminar. The poor woman did not know that the groom snored like a steam engine. After a while, the lady could not stand the locomotive and left for her mother's place. She wrote to him from Mumbai: "My love may be blind but not deaf."

The professor instructed his wife after dinner: "You must remind me tomorrow morning to take my notes to college as I have a lot in my mind and may forget."

Sure enough his wife forgot and said at the breakfast table, "I forgot what I was supposed to remember, but if you remember, don't forget."

Then, this is the story of two married teachers, who quarrelled one evening and vowed not to speak to each other. The husband had an early class and so he wrote a note and pinned it to the wife's pillow: "Wake me up at 6 a.m."

Next morning, the wife leaving for her own class pinned a note to her husband's pillow: "It is time to get up and get ready."

The professor came back home after classes and switched on the hall light. He found the light faint and the bulbs glowing feebly. He switched on the dining room light—here too the bulb glowed feebly, the same in the bedroom and the bathroom. Thinking that there was something wrong with the voltage, he called the campus electrician, who found that there was no problem and all the lights were okay. Then he noticed that the professor still had his sun goggles on.

"Oh," said the professor, taking off the glasses, "sorry."

Attending a short course at the University of Sussex, an Indian student and a Saudi Arabian were put in the same digs. Both were recently married and had left their wives home. "My wife is very beautiful," boasted the Indian, taking out his wedding photograph. "So is mine," averred the Saudi and fished out a photograph showing a beaming young man in wedding finery with his bride by the side covered from head to toe-nails in a black silken *burqua*.

The professor's wife was lean and thin but her sister was very corpulent. One day, the sister came to borrow from his wife a silk sari. After the sister left, the professor muttered to his wife: "You are so thin and she is so fat. How do you think your sari is going to fit her?"

The absent-minded professor was told by his wife: "Have you noticed that the baby has started walking?"

"Since when?"

"About a week."

"Oh, then he must have gone quite far away."

My professor keeps three glasses, one for near-sightedness, the second for farsightedness, and the third to look for the other two.

The lecturer of biology insisted on absolute punctuality and did not tolerate any tardiness. One morning, a student rushed into his class, five minutes late. "This is intolerable," shouted the lecturer.

"Sir, I was waiting in queue to buy your latest text book."

Surveying the class, the lecturer expostulates, "Well, then, why weren't the rest of you late?"

Newly arrived as a Humboldt fellow in Heidelberg, Germany, I lost the way to my digs. Since my German was inadequate, I stood on the street and was wondering whom to approach for directions, when I saw a Sikh gentleman crossing the street. I eagerly ran to him and told him my problem in Hindi. After giving directions, he asked me in all seriousness, "How did you guess that I was an Indian?"

The professor was deep in his work but suddenly remembered something. He called the gardener: "Go and water the plants."

"But it is raining," protested the *mali*.

"Don't argue. Take an umbrella," shouted the don.

The Institute of Fashion & Design was holding a counselling for admission to their first year course. The teacher asked the candidate: "What imaginative and creative work have you done so far?"

Producing his bio-data the candidate said: "Here is the proof, sir."

Two highly intellectual persons were exchanging notes. One of them said, "I got married as I was tired of washing my clothes, eating in restaurants and wearing socks with holes."

"Funny," replied his friend. "I got divorced for the same reasons."

The widowed lecturer of social sciences and the divorcee professor of homescience tied the knot. After some years, a common refrain heard in the household was: "Your children and my children are quarrelling with our children."

Here is a great professor, who stands before his class and declaims: "I have nothing to say, but I want to say it anyway."

My professor of physics lost a leg in an accident. An eternal optimist that he was, he quipped: "Now I can save money because I will have to buy a single shoe instead of a pair."

The wife of the philosophy professor was very concerned about the erratic behaviour of her husband and went to consult a psychologist. "I am very upset, doctor," said the woman, "my husband seems to be wandering in his mind."

"Don't let that worry you," the doctor replied. "I know your husband. He can't go far."

A certain professor of physics, with a large bee in his bonnet, lost the Lok Sabha election, but not relishing being out of power, he managed to get into the Rajya Sabha. A wag remarked wryly: "In physics, if an apple drops from a tree, it falls to the ground. But in politics, the apple sometimes bounces back to the tree."

Rotten apple?

Two impoverished teachers met in the staffroom. One said: "My wife had a dream last night that she was married to a millionaire."

The other remarked with a sigh: "You are lucky. My wife always thinks that in the day time."

This happened at a conference on fiscal reforms. Professor Naidu set forth the main points covering all aspects of the problem, and his speech was received with great appreciation. Now Professor Rajan was about to follow him but had the same views and found that Professor Naidu had covered all the points, and he had nothing more to say. So, this worthy man got up and said: "Before this meeting, Professor Naidu and I decided to trade speeches. He has just delivered mine and I am grateful for the reception you have accorded it. I regret I have misplaced his speech and can't remember a thing he intended to say." Rajan then sat down to a thunderous applause.

A conference-savvy academician says: "I never wear the name tag that is found in the conference kit that is handed out to me, for everyone will know exactly who I am when I fall asleep."

At a seminar on family planning, a demographer was reeling out statistics: "A woman somewhere in India is giving birth to a child every two seconds." An agitated woman in the audience shouted, "Then why not one of you go, find her and stop her."

A lecturer, who had a glad eye for a pretty face but was a bore, was holding forth in the staff club: "I am not in favour of the institution of marriage."

"No," remarked a long-suffering faculty: "That's right. Even your father didn't marry." And walked out.

The professor of psychology told his students to imagine that it was a war with Pakistan, and the last plane to leave Karachi was about to take off. The students were to persuade the guard at the bottom of the steps that they had to get on the crowded plane. Each student made a passionate plea. One said that she was pregnant, another that he had to report to the president, a third that he was required in the defence ministry. All pleas failed. Finally, one student ran up to the guard and screamed, "I just have to get on the plane. I am the pilot."

You now know, who made it to the plane.

Professor Singh was visiting England and wanted to motor down from London to Leeds. So he phoned the tourist office.

"Please let me know the distance from London to Leeds."

"272 miles," he was informed by the inquiry officer.

Professor: "And the distance from Leeds to London?"

"272 miles."

"Thank you so much," said the Professor. Inquiry officer: "For what?"

Professor: "Oh! That's because I thought I had to pay more to travel from Leeds to London than from London to Leeds?"

This is told by Sir Hugh Casson in *Raise Your Glasses:* When Charles II visited St. John's College, Oxford, he asked whether he could have a certain portrait of Charles I, but the college demurred.

"I will grant you any favour in return," said Charles.

"In that case," said the college, "it is yours."

"Thank you," said the King, "and what is your request?"

"Give it back, please," they said.

He did, and the portrait is still in the college library.

Wives of two university teachers were comparing notes on their husbands.

Said one very proudly, "He can talk on any subject under the sun."

Not to be outdone, the second boasted, "My husband can do better. He does not even need a subject and can talk, talk and talk."

The discussion veered round to the age-old problem: Which came first, the egg or the chicken?

Beant Singh got tired and finally expostulated: "You duffers, it is simple, you will get what you order first."

And finally: Old professors never die; they lose their faculties.

II

Examination Agony

It is rumoured that some examining bodies in the country are preparing two sets of papers for all examinations—one set for leaking and another for holding the re-examination.

The CBI was making enquiries about leakage of question papers from the Registrar's office. When shown some papers, the Registrar was indignant. "We are not responsible for these fake question papers. Whatever is leaked from here is absolutely genuine."

The younger brother of the University union president was doing his BA papers in a corner of the Controller of Examination's office. Asked why this special arrangement for a candidate, the controller explained: "I have to personally watch that he gets into no problems."

The don in Patna jail, accused of leaking exam papers is fighting the general elections. He has published a manifesto assuring that if elected, he will introduce a bill making copying in examinations, a fundamental right.

The history-sheeter was standing outside the gate of the examination hall and chatting with the invigilators. Inside, mass copying was going on merrily. The jeep of the proctor slowed down before the hall, and then accelerated away.

Questioned, the proctor quipped: "Just for a few sheets, I have no intention of becoming history!"

A student would take the pen to write and then with a frown put it down and stare at the question paper. An invigilator, who was watching the antics for sometime went over and asked, "Are some questions bothering you?"

"No," was the reply. "It is the answers that are troubling me."

A teacher urging students to prepare for the final exam tells them that the time was running out as the paper had been set and sent to the printers. He asks, "Are there any questions?"

"Yes," enquires a student, "who is the printer?"

The principal of a school in Uttar Pradesh was being felicitated by the Education Department for the unique achievement of a hundred percent result in the High School Examination and all candidates having secured first class with distinctions. Trying to be modest, he remarked that such an achievement would not have been possible but for the cooperation of the teachers, who spared no effort in supplying the correct answers to the candidates!

Two students were late for the examination. They hurriedly made up an excuse: "We had a flat tyre."

The examiner put them in different rooms, and among the questions, he asked was, "Which tyre?"

A father promised his wayward son that he would be rewarded with a bike if he passed his BA exam but he failed. The father remonstrated his son that despite the offer of a bike, he had failed. The excuse of the son was, "I was learning how to ride a bike and so could not concentrate on studies."

The young girl had been wasting her time during the semester and when the examination time came near, she was unprepared. She went to the handsome tutor and said, "I would do anything if you passed me."

"Really? Anything?" he enquired.

"Yes, anything," was the excited response.
"Then go and study hard."

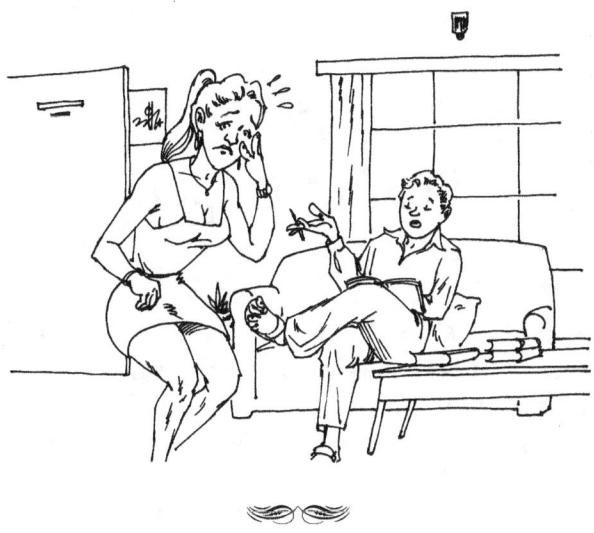

The maths lecturer was set to start the unit test. "Now," he announced, "I am very democratic, and therefore, I would like to give you a choice. You may write a three-hour test, or three tests of one hour each. Which do you want?"

The class looked back in silence, unable to decide which one was the lesser evil. A boy took the decision for the class. "Please, sir," he proposed, "I would rather fail in one test than in three."

In the examination hall, Bunta suddenly started to undress. Astonished, the invigilator asked: "Bunta, why are you taking off your clothes?" Replied Bunta: "Sir, it says here, **Answer in brief.**"

III
School Capers

Driving her car one morning, a woman overshot a stop sign. She was stopped by a police officer, who recognized her as his former English teacher. "Madam," he said, "those stop signs are full stops, not commas."

A schoolma'am asked the inspector at the gate, "Which platform for the local to Kanpur?"

The inspector replied, "Ma'am, if you turned left you will be right." Recognising him as one of her former pupils, she chided, "Don't be cheeky, young man."

"Ma'am, then if you turned right you will be left," he quipped.

The school teacher was speeding and was stopped by a policeman. Seeing it was his former teacher, the bobby didn't give her a *chaalan* and advised: "Drive safe."

"Say, *safely*." Commented the teacher.
"What?"

"You have corrected my driving and I am correcting your grammar."

The student wrote 'untill', and the teacher advised her: "There is a single 'l' in 'until'. Correct the spelling."

"Do I remove the first 'l' or the second?" queried the pupil.

The teacher was taking a class of modern English poetry. One student seemed puzzled. "How come the poet uses capital letters in the middle of a sentence and misspells some of the words?" she wanted to know.

"This is called poetic licence," the teacher explained.

"Oh," the student asked, "how can I apply for one?"

An NCC cadet impatiently waiting for the marching practice to end, kept sneaking repeated glances at his watch. Suddenly, a furious instructor thundered, "What are you doing?"

"Marking time, sir," came the prompt reply.

To the question, "Which noun is trousers?" One boy came up with the following answer: "It is an uncommon noun. It is single at the top and plural at the bottom."

The teacher was telling the virtue of consulting a thesaurus. After the lecture, he asked a student: "What is a synonym?"

One bright scholar answered: "It is a word you use when you can't spell the other one."

As he goes through the report card, a father's frown dissolves into anger. "Such miserable marks deserve a sound thrashing."

The son answers: "Fine, *papa*, I know where the teacher lives."

Ramu: Do you think anyone can tell the future with cards?

Shyamu; My mother can tell.

Ramu: How can you say?

Shyamu: She took one look at my report card and told me what would happen when my father got home.

After a lecture on humour in American literature, the professor asks: "Who is Dorothy Parker?"

Promptly answers a student: "The proprietor of Parker pens."

Teacher: Ramu, what is your favourite breakfast cereal?

Ramu: "Serial, Sir? *Kyunki Saas Bhi Kabhi Bahu Thee.*

Teacher: You failed the English test. Did you read my book?

Govinda: Sir, I did not fail because I read your book but because I was ill.

"I don't think that I did so badly in the test that you gave me a zero," complained the pupil.

"I agree that you did not deserve a zero, but I don't know a figure lower than that," countered the teacher.

In the moral science class, the teacher advised that you should say nothing about the dead unless you say something good.

Student: "Even about Veerappan?"
Teacher: "Yes."
Student: "He is dead. GOOD."

Teacher: Rita, you made the same mistakes in the answers as Sita sitting next to you. What do you have to say about this.

Rita: We both have the same teacher.

Child: Why do they call our language, the mother tongue?

Father: Because fathers seldom get a chance to use it.

Beant Singh was participating in a quiz programme in his school in Ludhiana.

The quiz master asked: "How much is two plus two?"

Beant: "Twenty-two."

Master: "Wrong. But I give you another chance."

Beant: "Six."

Master: "Wrong again. However, I give you one final chance."

Beant: "Four."

Before the quiz master could say anything, the audience chanted: "Give him another chance. Give him one more chance."

The English department announced a special class on 'creative writing'. Buta Singh wanted to enroll and asked the professor the duration of the course. "Twelve months," was the reply.

When Buta got the enrolment form, the duration was stated 'one year'. Buta was upset and complained to the teacher: "You told me that the course will last twelve months but the form says 'one year'. I can't spend such a long time taking this course."

Teacher: Let me hear how far you can count.

Ramu: One, two, three, four, five, six, seven, eight, nine, ten, jack, queen, king.

Teacher: "I am taking all my forty children to the zoo today."

"Forty? You have forty. . ."exclaims a shocked bystander.

"Yes, I am their class teacher."

A natural history teacher takes her class to the top of the hill to emphasise the peace and quietness of the place. "Keep still and listen to the silence," says she.

After a while one student whispers to another, "I don't hear anything, can you?"

The school picnic was in a row boat watching the splendours of the setting sun on the horizon. Suddenly, Buta Singh shouts: "Let's row closer to the sun to watch it better."

Dinesh: I need to borrow your pencil.

Ganesh: You know what Polonius said: Neither a borrower nor lender be.

Dinesh: Point this kid to me and I will teach him to mind his own business.

After an argument with the principal, the English teacher came to the class and rested her head on the desk. One child asked, what was the matter?

Without raising her head, the teacher uttered only one word: "Tense."

Thy child recited: "You were tired, you are tired, you will be tired."

Some mischievous kids bring a donkey to the class. The teacher enters, surveys the scene and says: "Boys, I see there is one more of you today."

An inquisitive 10-year-old asks her father: "Daddy, tell me, how eclipses of the sun occur?"

Father scratches his head and after some thought, replies: "Er, I don't know."

"Then tell me, daddy, the height of Mt. Everest."

The same scratching of the head and reply: "I don't know."

Two more questions are asked and the reply is the same. The girl folds up her notebook and starts to leave.

"Where are you going? If you don't ask questions, how will you learn anything?" admonishes her father.

At a contest held during a Delhi college-leaving social, a group of girls were asked the question: "Would you marry an immensely rich man with no brains or a brilliant man with little money." The one good, who got the prize, said, "I'll take the rich one, because I have got the brains."

A former minister of education with antediluvian ideas had introduced *Jjyotirvigyan* and *Purohitya* courses as subjects in universities that required a good knowledge of Sanskrit. But this ancient language is not easily mastered and was causing problems for students. Here is the lament of a scholar parodied from an old ditty:

> Sanskrit is a language
> As dead as it can be.
> It killed the ancient Hindus,
> And now, it is killing me.

An inspector of schools went to the Hindi class and asked a question. "You have been taught the *Ramayana*. Tell me, who broke Shiva's bow?"

There was silence all around After a while, one boy raised his hand and said, "Sir, I don't know who did it, but it wasn't me."

The inspector turned to the teacher and admonished him for not doing his job properly. The teacher said, "Rest assured, sir, I will find out, who broke it and let you know."

In disgust, the inspector called the headmaster and narrated the whole story. The headmaster was contrite, and told the inspector, "Boys will be boys, sir. Please forget the matter, and I will see that no bows are broken in future."

The warden was in the habit of taking a round of the hostel at odd hours. After one of his silent visits, late at night, the resident wag next door peeped in my room and whispered, "You know, Professor Dar passed away peacefully."

Buta was terribly indolent and failed in his class, three years in succession. The principal was disgusted and asked Buta to go and find a job. Buta wanted a certificate. Not wishing to hurt Buta but also not wishing to give a false certificate, the principal wrote: "Any employer will be very lucky if he makes Buta work for him."

Students of geography of the Dibrugarh University were taken in an excursion to the Majuli Island, the largest riverine island in the world in the

Brahmaputra river. Standing on the southern embankment, one student wanted to know from the teacher whether the water went around the entire island.

The teacher gave her class a maths problem involving a leaking tap. She noticed that one pupil had written a number that appeared quite senseless. "What does this number mean?" she asked.

"It is the phone number of our plumber," was the sagacious reply.

At the kindergarten, the four-year old was being taught the basics of addition. "What is one apple plus one apple?" asked the teacher.

"Two apples," said the child after a brief thought.

"Good. Now tell me, what's two apples plus one more apple?"

"Much better," was the prompt response.

Buta was playing all the time and was not doing well in the class. So his mother reprimanded him. "Buta," she said, "I wish that you'd pay a little attention to your studies."

"But I do, Mom," Buta replied. "I pay as little attention to it as possible."

Teacher: There will be an eclipse of the moon, this evening. You all must watch it.

Krishnu: Which channel?

India is a cricket crazy nation. So, no wonder that this happened.

In a Bible class, the teacher asked where was the Garden of Eden and what was it known for.

One child answered promptly: "Eden Garden is in Calcutta and it is a famous cricket ground."

Art Master: Radha, I asked you to draw a horse and a cart, but you have drawn only the horse.

Radha: Yes, sir. The horse will draw the cart.

Two teachers went to the *dhaba* near the school and ordered two teas. Then they produced sandwiches from their *jholas* and started to eat. The owner came over and told them: "You can't eat your own sandwiches in here."

The teachers looked at each other, shrugged their shoulders and exchanged their sandwiches.

The teacher was telling the story of how Archimedes discovered the principle of specific gravity that is named after him. "One day, he noticed that when he got into the bath, the water rose displacing the water equal to his body volume. He ran down the street, naked, shouting "Eureka, eureka!" The teacher asked whether any one in the class knew what 'eureka' meant.

One in the class took a wild guess: "I am naked, I am naked!"

The English teacher asked a student, "Give me a synonym for injustice."

"When my father makes a mistake in the homework and the teacher blames me."

February 2004 had 29 days instead of the usual 28. The teacher explained that every fourth year, they added one day to the month of February.

"So, by the year 2020, February will have 33 days," said the third-grader after some mental calculation.

Student: "Papa, will you please help me with my homework?"

Father: "I am sorry, but it won't be right."

Student: "Well, at least you could try."

Mother was shocked. Mugging up, the four-year-old was repeating to herself, "Two and two, the son-of-a-bitch is four."

The next day, the mother confronted the teacher, who was equally mystified. The pupil was asked to repeat what she was memorising. Then the teacher burst out laughing. The child was told to remember that "Two and two, *the sum of which* is four."

The little girl asked her friend to come and play in the evening. "No I can't," called her friend from the window. "If I don't watch papa, he won't do my homework."

Johnny of New York was not getting any help from his father in doing his homework. He announced: "Dad, I think I will outsource my homework to India."

Punjab Agricultural University at Ludhiana prefers to admit students from within the state. A column in the admission form asks: "Length of residence." Buta Singh from Patiala filled in: About 100 kms."

With great annoyance, the teacher asked a boy: "Why do you always answer a question with a question?"
"Well, why not?" he countered.

With an air of innocence, Rita asked: "Daddy, can you write with your eyes closed?"

"I could try. But why?"

"Then sign this," said Rita, thrusting forward her report card.

The class was taken to the circus. One little girl was asked how did she enjoy the visit. "Fine. But I did not think much of the man who threw knives at the woman."

"But why not?"

"He missed every time he threw a knife," replied the little girl.

Teacher: Which is farther away, England or the moon?

Ramesh: England.

Teacher: England? What makes you think so?

Ramesh: Because we can see the moon but we can't see England.

Teacher: Find Australia on the map for me, Anand.

Anand: It's there on the bottom of the map.

Teacher: That's right. Now, Gopal, who discovered Australia?

Gopal: Anand, sir.

The master was very annoyed with the careless ways of a boy. He pointed with his cane and said, "There is a great lazy bum at the end of this stick."

"Which end, sir?" asked the cheeky boy.

Teacher: We will have only a half-day of school, this morning.

Class: Hurrah!

Teacher: We will have the other half, this afternoon.

A child wanted to join the swimming class in the school, but the mother would not agree to it. She said, "I will not let you enter the water until you know swimming"

A three-year-old went to a kindergarten where all the staff wore identical aprons.

When her mother asked what she thought of the teachers, she replied, "They all have the same body but different heads."

These days, freebies are being offered with all kinds of merchandise. Tired after a hectic shopping, a mother buys a bottled water to quench her thirst. On the bottle are printed 'BACTERIA FREE' under the brand name. The little girl tugs at her mother's saree, and whispers: "You haven't taken the free bacteria, Mummy".

This was long, long back. I was coaching my grade III daughter for her history examination. I told her to remember that India became independent in 1947, the same year she was born. Sure enough, she was asked this question.

Her prompt answer was: "India became independent in the year I was born."

Arun's doting mother admitted him to a play school. She gave the teacher a long list of instructions, and the final was: "Don't ever punish him. Just slap the boy next to him, that will frighten Arun."

The teacher asked a little girl, "Why did Robinhood rob the rich?"

The girl thought for a while and replied: "Because the poor didn't have any money."

A kid came home from a prep school and told her mother, "Mom, guess what? We learned today how to make babies?"

Shoked, mother kept her cool. "That's interesting." She asked, "And how do you make babies?"

"Simple. Just change **y** to **i** and add **es**, answered the kid sharply.

Renu was composing a letter to her cousin and taking a long time. Her mother asked: "Renu, why are you writing the letter so slowly?"

"Because Manju is just learning to read and cannot read very fast."

The solicitous neighbour asked the father: "How does your son stand in the class?"

"Usually in the corner," replied the father.

Teacher: "Why are you so sad?"

Boy: "I requested my father for money to buy books, but he sent the books instead."

IV
Science Panorama

Nobel laureate C.V. Raman, who discovered an important optical phenomenon which is named after him as the 'Raman Effect', was a strict teetotaller. Once, in Paris, at the 25th anniversary celebration of his discovery, he was offered a glass of champagne. "You may know the Raman Effect on alcohol," he said while refusing the drink, "but I certainly won't let you see the alcohol effect on Raman."

Einstein was travelling by tram in his hometown in Germany and had an argument about the change after paying the fare. The exasperated conductor shouted: "Go and learn some basic arithmetic."

The teacher asked the science class: "Give me an example of how heat expands things and cold contracts them?"
A bright kid raised her hand immediately.

"The days are much longer in summer than in winter" was the sharp reply.

Sir Issac Newton, the great scientist to whom is attributed the discovery of *gravity*, commissioned a carpenter to make a shelter for his cats in the backyard. He asked the carpenter to make two holes for the cats to get in and out: A small one for the kitten and a larger one for the big tabby.

Albert Einstein was once asked to explain his *Theory of Relativity* in simple terms for a layman to understand. "When a man sits with a pretty girl for an hour, it seems like a minute. But let him sit on a hot stove for a minute and it's longer than an hour. That's relativity," he explained.

In a science class, the teacher boils some water in a beaker. When the water makes a bubbling noise, he asks: "Why is the water making this noise?"

A back-bencher volunteers an answer: "That's the germs screaming before being killed."

Professor Misra was travelling to Roorkee to take a practical examination. In the evening, he opened his dinner packet and after finishing packet, he threw the empty packet out of the train, saving the rubber band for possible use in future. When he got back home, his wife wanted back the silver spoon that she had kept in the dinner packet.

Then the professor realized that he had thrown away the spoon along with the soiled packet though he had saved the worthless rubber band.

The chauffeur of a famous scientist hearing the same lectures had it by heart. Tired one day, the scientist asked his chauffeur to take his place while he sat in the last row of the auditorium with his face covered. The chauffeur's lecture went quite well, and at the end, he asked if there were any questions.

"Yes," said a member of the audience and asked a highly technical question. Panic-stricken for a moment, the chauffeur recovered his wits and replied, "Oh, this is an easy one and I will let my chauffeur answer it." Saying this, he pointed towards the scientist.

A newly-awarded PhD scholar attended a seminar where he had to present a research paper. Not used to public speaking, he was very nervous and decided to read through his written communication. However, he could not comprehend why people suddenly laughed in the middle of his presentation. He came to know later that he had also spoken out the P.T.Os at the end of each page, while reading out.

The United States government spent a few million dollars trying to develop a pen that would work in the zero-gravity of an astronaut's capsule, but without success. Frustrated, they approached the Soviet space agency.

"Simple," they replied, "We use pencils."

A professor of zoology kept his crabs in an open tank. On being asked whether he was not afraid that they might escape, he replied, "They are Indian crabs. No sooner one starts climbing up, another will immediately claw it back. There is no danger of one climbing high enough to the top and escaping."

A boy was caught eating during biology lesson. The teacher asked him angrily, "What do you think you are doing?"

He replied, "A practical experiment on digestion."

A student, who thought he was very smart took different parts from various insects and glued them together. He took the creation to Charles Darwin, the famous naturalist, and requested him to identify the insect.

"Did it hum when you caught it?" asked the scientist.

"Yes, it did," enthused the smart one.

"Then, it's a humbug."

The chemistry professor at Lucknow University wanted to bring home to the students the virtue of observation. So, one day, he takes a beaker containing urine to the class. He invites the class to sample it and tell the taste. None in the class accepts his offer. Then the teacher dips his finger in the beaker and licks it saying, "If I can do it, why not you?" Then, some students pick up enough courage and follow the teacher.

After a few students have tasted the urine with disgust written large on their faces, the professor remonstrates them, "Gentlemen, if you had only been observant, you would have noticed that I put my forefinger in the beaker but licked the middle finger.

The famous ornithologist, Salim Ali employed a fresh zoology graduate as his assistant. He was taken on field trips but his powers of observation were woeful and he could not comprehend even simple instructions. Before letting him go, Ali told him: "Sorry, you could never be a bird-watcher because you are birdbrained."

Geochronicle

This is a sage advice: Never lend money to a geologist for you will never get it back because to a geologist, a million years is just, 'Recent'.

The geology teacher was organizing a field trip for which tents were being kept ready. One student, who was allotted a damaged tent, complained. Off handed, the teacher asked, "Does it leak?"

The sufferer replied sarcastically: "No. But only when it rains."

The examiner asked the age of a fossil.

Student: Sixty-five million and three years.

Examiner: How can you date it so precisely?

Student: When I joined the class, the professor told me it was sixty-five million years old, and that was three years back.

Do you know why geologists like the movie, *Basic Instinct*? Because the actress, Sharon Stone is acting in it!

Decades back, perhaps, before Word War II, I had purchased a globe and it was lost with other junk. My son, a geology student, recently retrieved it and observed that it was useless now.

"Why," I asked.

"Continental drift." he remarked pithily.

The wife wanted divorce from her geologist husband. The ground? "He is always finding some fault or the other."

This was a basic course in mountaineering where people from various streams of life were participating. The camp cook asked one of the participants: "What is your profession?"

""I am a geologist."

"Ha, you're the right man. Please pick out the stones from the rice."

The professor of physical geography asked the student, who was getting married during the summer vacation: "Do you intend to have your honeymoon in Finland?"

"I think not. There is no night for six months," was the pragmatic reply.

After a survey, it was found that the favourite rock music group of geologists was 'Rolling Stones'.

Question: Do you know what is the favourite sport of a geologist?
Answer: Hammer throw.

There is no dearth of bright students. A student examining fossils in the geology museum asks his instructor: "Sir, are these fossils of living or dead plants?"

Cyber Symphony

While browsing in a bookshop, a woman asked a salesman where the computer section was located. The salesman directed her to the back of the shop and asked, "Is there something specific that you are looking for?"

"Yes," replied the woman, "my husband."

Advised to use Roman numerals to number his thesis chapters, the scholar said, "But my keyboard doesn't have Roman numerals on it."

A man boasted that he writes things which the whole world reads: Stuff that elicits strong emotions from people all over, makes them scream, cry, howl in pain and anger..

Actually, he writes error messages for the Microsoft.

The conference rooms at the offices of the Internet giant Yahoo have names like Coherent, Disposed, Consistent and Definite. This way, if someone asks, "Where is John?" you can say, "Oh, he's in coherent", or "He's in disposed", or "He's in consistent", or "He's indefinite.

After being involved in a serious accident, a man was rushed to the hospital. When he regained consciousness, the doctor asked his name.
"Kishore Bhandari, the man replied."
"And your address?"
kbhandari09@yahoo.com

Three Microsoft scientists were on a long car trip when they got a flat tyre. They stopped and studied the situation. The sales manager said, "What we need is a new car." The service guy said, "Wait, let us switch some parts around until it works again." The software engineer said, "No, just turn the car on and off a few times to see if that fixes the problem."

He came back home all fagged out, flung himself on the bed and called out to his wife: "I have fever and I possibly got the viral from my computer."

A computer engineer went on a long trip. He sent this e-mail to his wife:

"Brought hardware and software but forgot underwear. Courier them at once."

He was very busy solving a problem on the computer and had no time even to eat. His wife brought him a plate of sandwiches and urged him to take bites as he worked. He assured her, "I will delete them promptly."

As he passed the site of a car accident, a computer programmer remarked, "The brake disk drive crashed."

His parents bought a computer and e-mailed him: "This is really going to be fun." The boy groaned: "I don't know about that, but now I have parents at home and in cyberspace too."

The effect of computers on young children was brought home to me recently by my four-year old son. A visitor asked him to spell his name. Of course, I can—A-M-R-I-T ... enter.

Buta goes to a shop selling furnishing materials and demands to see some drapes. "Show me some curtains for my computer."

"For your computer?"

"You see, I have installed **Windows** on my computer."

When he had a computer problem, Beant Singh was advised to go to the menu bar. So he started his mobike and headed straight for the nearby Chandni Bar and asked for the menu card.

Question: What do you do when the computer overheats?

Answer: Open all the **Windows.**

Beant had frustration written large on his face, and so Jaswant asked him what was the matter? "I am trying to download gold from **www.goldmine.com** but without any success."

A programmer fed a complicated data in the computer but got an instant answer. The chap fed the same data to recheck and got the same answer, but a line was printed at the bottom of the screen:

YOU ASS, THE ANSWER IS NOT GOING TO CHANGE.

"**H**ow many genders are there?" An Internet-addicted child was asked by the teacher.

"Three: Male, female and e-mail," said the bright one on the computer.

Question: What is the thing that travels faster than e-mail?

Reply: "Gossip."

A proverb of the cyber time:

Give a man a fish and you feed him for a day; teach him to use the 'net' and he won't bother you for weeks.

Complains an employee about his boss:
 "His **byte** is worse than his bark."

Old saws resharpened:
 "The mouse is mightier than the pen."
 "A picture is worth a megabyte."
 "The e-mail of the species is more deadly than the snail-mail."
 "C:\ is the root cause of all directories."
 "Pentium wise and pen-and-paper foolish."
 "Too many clicks spoil the browse."
 "The geek shall inherit the earth."
 "Don't byte off more than what you have on your disk."
 "To err is human, but to really foul up things, you require a computer."

Motto on the door of a cyber café:
 "In **Gates**, we trust."

To the present-day kid, computer lingo comes very easily. The mother opens a book and asks the child which story she wants to be read to her. Says the kid: "I don't know. Let's open the main menu and see what stories are in the book." Amused, the mother opens the **Table of Contents** and shows her.

A computer is almost human—except that it does not blame its mistakes on another computer.

A comment in the papers:
"The rumour spread far and wide by the word of mouse."

You will know a computer geek when a man does something nice to his motherboard on the **Mother's Day**.

Latest office gossip:
The boss has got a new laptop, curvaceous and blonde with a notebook.

The computer-age seven-year-old saw her grandfather pounding away on his manual typewriter. "Gee!" she said, "there is no monitor and your keyboard has a printer attached."

A sage advice:
"Don't *curser* when your wife doesn't get your breakfast in time.

He had a friend come over for coffee and *gup-shup*. His four-year-old daughter asked: "Papa, what were you telling uncle?"

"Oh, nothing in particular. We were just chatting."

"But where was your laptop?" queried the cyber-age child.

A kindergarten teacher was playing the favourite game of the tiny-tots by asking them to make sounds that different animals made.

The dog barks: "Bow-wow."

The cat says: "Meow."

And for the mouse, one bright one said: "Click."

The wife of an Internet addict confides to her friend: "Only I know how I am *surferring* him."

An advice given by a software vendor to a customer:

"You must first upgrade your downloaded software in order to download our upgraded software.

Question: Do you know that a computer can work faster than a human?

Answer: Because it doesn't have to answer the phone.

The day is not far when you will get a message like this:

"Hello, I am the computer. So far nobody else knows that you haven't paid your grocery bill, but if you don't pay within a week, I will put it on the **Net**."

Heard at the Infosys tennis court:

"You need to practise your back-space drive."

VII
Bibliophile

There are many practitioners of this philosophy. One conversation goes like this:
　　Raman: I would like to borrow this book.
　　Krishnan: I don't lend my books to anyone.
　　Raman: But I promise to return it soon.
　　Krishnan: It is only on this promise that I have built up my library.

In an American University, there is a stone tablet in front of the library on which are etched the names of some of the greatest minds of Western civilization: Plato, Aristotle, Virgil, Homer, Sophocles, Demosthenes. "I wonder," mused a professor, "why the name of Socrates is missing from the list?"
　　"Simple," explained a colleague, "he never published."

A scholar goes into a bookshop and asks the assistant: "Where is the self-help section?"

"If I told you, it would defeat your whole purpose."

Customer: Do you have a book titled *Man, the Master of Women*?

Salesgirl: The fiction section is on the back.

Dale Carnegie's book, *How to Win Friends And Influence People* has been a classic of its kind and has sold millions of copies since it was first published in the thirties of the last century. A scholar recently saw a copy in the college bookstore and wanted to buy it. As he reached for it, a brash undergraduate snatched it away from him shouting, "I want it—I saw it first." To his surprise, the salesgirl, handed over the copy to the grim-faced youngster, who paid and walked out with it.

Before he could remonstrate, the girl said, "Sorry, it is the only copy in stock but I gave it to him because I felt he needed it. Don't you agree?"

There are books and books, and readers and readers. A young man was asked: "What books, apart from the *Gita* and the *Ramayana*, have helped you the most?"

"My mother's cook book and my father's cheque book," replied he.

I was watching a beauty parade on the TV—one girl more beautiful than the other. "Ah!" I thought. "A thesaurus of beauties."

Mother did not want her sixteen-year-old daughter to start reading murder mysteries and so she rummaged through her pile of books and removed a book of blood-thirsty melodrama full of murder and suicide in which one fellow murders his brother and takes over his brother's job and wife.

The book was William Shakespeare's *Hamlet.*

A recent incumbent of the Raj Bhawan—the erstwhile Government House—went on an inspection tour of the magnificent colonial building. He took out a few books from the well-stocked but musty library. "Hmm, I see that this book is dated 1789 and this 1802, and this 1813..."

"What are these old books doing in the library. Throw them away and buy new ones," he ordered.

One of the books of P.G. Wodehouse, the famous humourist, has this dedication:

"To my wife, without whose absence this book could not have been written."

This is a truism propounded by Maxim Gorky: "Writers build castles in the air, readers live in them, and publishers collect the rent."

The lexicographer looks into the eyes of his beloved and says: "You are like a dictionary—you add meaning to my life."

For a sales Ad in the local paper put in by a college lecturer:

"Encyclopaedia Britannica for Sale. Excellent condition. No longer required. Wife knows everything."

The salesman was stealing **books** from the store. He was finally caught and was **booked** by the police.

A book of 300 pages published by the State Text Book Corporation has 150 pages of *Errata*.

The dedication of Morrie Ryskind's book *Unaccustomed as I Am* reads: "To the Great American Democracy—May It Bring Me Royalty."

Beant Singh slams down a thick tome on the return counter of the library and says in disgust: "This book is worthless; it contains only a lot of names and all kinds of numerals but no reading matter."

"So, it is you, who took away the phone directory," exclaims the library clerk!

Reviews of some books are very pithy—short, but not sweet, but they say it all. Some examples:

"This is an out-of-this world book—and should stay there."

"This book has a beginning, a middle, and an end, but not in the same order."

"The book is a thorough muck; the only redeeming feature is its wide, clean margins."

"Once you put it down, don't pick it up."

The absent-minded physics professor was browsing through the bookshop's science section when he saw a new book on the subject of quantum mechanics. He bought the volume and reaching home unwrapped the purchase.

It was a book that he himself had written.

One woman: "Is your husband a bookworm?"
Second woman: "No, an ordinary one."

A wag describes an autobiography as an obituary in serial form with the last 'instalment missing.

This is the story of Khuda Bux Khan, the founder of Patna's Oriental Library of priceless manuscripts and paintings. He was not averse to pinching a good book whenever and wherever, he could. His justification. "There are three kinds of blind men: Those who cannot see; those careless enough to lend books even to friends; and those, who return books, they borrowed.

A young mother goes into a bookstore. "I would like a book on child education," she enquires.

"I am sorry," replies the salesgirl, "but we don't have one in the stock."

"Then I would like one on the art of self control."

VIII
Author! Author!

Henry David Thoreau, the American poet, essayist and naturalist, once wrote a book titled, *A Week on the Ground and Merrimack Rivers* that did not sell many copies out of the 1000 printed. Thoreau bought the 706 unsold copies and recorded the transaction in his personal journal: "I have now a library of nearly nine hundred volumes, over seven hundred of which I wrote myself."

Historian Arthur Schlesinger, Jr. stopped the author, Liz Carpenter and said: "Liz, I liked your book. Who wrote it for you?"

"I am glad you liked it, Arthur," she countered: "Who read it to you?"

This is reproduced from *The Star,* Johannesburg:

The would-be author, Kenneth Phiri appealed to Zimbabwe's High Court not to send him to prison because he needed time to complete his book. But the presiding judge sent him to prison for four-and-a-half years for robbery and impersonating a police officer. "You will have to complete writing this book in prison," the judge told him.

The book's title: *Crime Does Not Pay*.

Sir Arthur C. Clarke and Isaac Asimov, both internationally famous science fiction writers, had a mock-hate relationship. When a plane crashed and many passengers survived, it turned out that one of the survivors had kept calm during the perilous attempts to land by reading a Clarke novel. This was reported in a news dispatch. Clark made numerous copies of the article and sent one to Asimov and at the bottom wrote: "What a pity, he didn't read one of your novels. He would have slept through the whole wretched ordeal."

"On the contrary," Asimov wrote back, "the reason he was reading your novel was that if the plane did crash, the death would come as a blessed relief."

Once G.K. Chesterton, who was very corpulent, met George Bernard Shaw, who was very lean, on the street and teased him: "Shaw, seeing you one would think that there was a famine in England."

Shaw's retort was swift: "And looking at you, Chesterton, one would know the cause of it."

The American writer, Dorothy Parker and the playwright, Clare Booth Luce approached a doorway at the same time. Luce stepped aside saying, "Age before beauty." Parker swept through the door, tartly retorting, "Pearl before swine."

Chesterton was reputed to be a bit absent-minded. Once on a trip, he wired his wife:
AM IN MARKET HARBOROUGH STOP WHERE OUGHT I TO BE.
Mrs. Chesterton replied:
HOME.

Browsing through a second-hand bookstall, Shaw came across a volume of his own plays that he had presented to a friend inscribed in his own hand. Buying the book, Shaw wrote under the inscription: "With renewed compliments, G.B.S.", and sent it back to the early recipient.

A famous beauty once told Shaw that if he married her, their children will have his brains and her beauty.

"No," countered Shaw, "what happens if they have your brains and my beauty?"

A writer was bragging about his ancestors. "My father was the lord of a manor, my grandfather was a general, my great-grandfather was..."

Shaw cut him short. "Enough. If you keep on tracing your ancestry backwards, you will have to end with the monkey."

When Cornelia Otis Skinner, the great actress, opened in a revival of Shaw's *Candida,* he cabled:
EXCELLENT GREATEST!
Miss Skinner, overwhelmed, cabled back:
UNDESERVING SUCH PRAISE.
Shaw replied:
I MEANT THE PLAY.
Miss Skinner bristled and wired back:
SO DID I.

Shaw was not the one to stand any suggestion about his work. A theatrical company touring New Zealand cabled him:
TRAIN SCHEDULES MAKE IT ESSENTIAL WE CUT LENGTH PERFORMANCE STOP CAN WE HAVE PERMISSION TO CUT EPILOGUE FROM ST JOAN
Shaw's pithy reply:
YOU HAVE MY PERMISSION TO CUT EPILOGUE PROVIDING YOU PERFORM IT ON TRAIN!

On a narrow country bridge coming from the opposite side, Shaw met another author who hated him. "I never give way to a scoundrel," said the other one. "But I always do," said Shaw and stepped aside to let him pass.

Shaw commenting on the suffragettes remarked, "Women cried: 'we will not be dictated to' and proceeded to become stenographers."

Shaw used to pay his monthly grocer's bill by cheque. The grocer was a smart guy and instead of encashing it, he would frame it and put it on display. If the cheque was for £5, the note under the display would say: "Cheque signed by George Bernard Shaw, £10." Sure enough, some passerby would notice it and buy it.

It is not known whether Shaw ever found this out.

Charles Lamb, the author of *Tales From Shakespeare*, was a notorious latecomer to office. His boss chided him one day: "Mr. Lamb, you come to the office late everyday."

Lamb replied, "But I make it up by going early."

And that was that.

British author, Noel Coward once encountered American novelist Edna Ferber, who was wearing a tailored suit. "You look almost like a man," observed Coward.

"So do you," retorted Ferber.

There was no love lost between the novelist William Faulkner and Ernest Hemingway. Faulkner, in a fit of pique, once described Hemingway: "He has never been known to use a word that might send a reader to the dictionary."

The famous banker, Henri de Rothschild told the author, Tristan Bernard: "People tell me you are very witty, so please make me laugh."

Bernard replied: "People tell me you're very rich, so please lend me 100,000 francs."

The famous French author, Victor Hugo wanted to know from his publisher how his recently published novel, *Les Misérables* was selling, and reportedly sent him a simple enquiry which read:

"?"

And received the expressive reply:

"!".

(This is recognized by *The Guinness Book of World Records* as the shortest correspondence.)

Mark Twain in his autobiography wrote a scathing tirade about a publisher, who had cheated him. But he ended with a note of forgiveness: "He's been dead for a quarter of a century now. I have only compassion for him and if I could send him a fan, I would."

At the promotional function of his book, an author started showing some fatigue as he doggedly autographed his latest book. The publisher's agent leaned over and whispered: "Keep going. Remember, they cannot return signed books."

It is not surprising that the strength of the author revived.

After sending the manuscript of his latest book, *Travels With My Aunt,* to his American publishers, novelist Graham Greene received the following cable: "Terrific book, but will need to change the title."

"No need to change the title," responded Greene. "Easier to change publishers." And he did just that.

Benjamin Disraeli, the 9th century British statesman and twice prime minister, quipped that "When I want to read a novel, I write one."

Robert Benchley, American humourist, once remarked: "It took me fifteen years to discover that I had no talent for writing, but I could not give up because by that time, I was too famous."

Someone asked the French novelist, Guy de Maupassant why he wrote stories only about fallen women.

"A virtuous woman is of no interest to anybody," was his obvious reply.

Ernest Hemingway, Nobel Prize-winning American novelist, was often short of ready cash but was very generous. A story is told about him that when short of funds, he would borrow 100 francs from the barmen at the Ritz, give it to them as a tip and promise to pay them back, the next week.

British author, Arnold Bennett was autographing copies of his books at a literary function. One avid fan of his had three first editions, but thought it impolite to get all the three signed by Bennett at one time. He presented the first one and rejoined the queue, trusting that the author won't remember, him. He did this thrice. At the last presentation, without a trace of a smile, Bennett wrote, "To..., who is fast becoming an old friend."

This was the comment of the novelist Henri Miller on a highly complimentary letter about one of his books: "I particularly prize your letter because it's a kind of letter I would have written myself, had I not been the author of the book."

American humourist Art Linkletter is probably the author of this profound observation: But for marriage, husbands and wives would have to fight with strangers.

"At last," announced a budding author with grim satisfaction, "I have written something that any magazine will be glad to accept."

"Good!" exclaimed his friend. "What is it?"

"A cheque for a year's subscription," was the response.

The noted social scientist, Bibhuti Sengupta was offloaded at Delhi from a flight to Mumbai as a cabinet minister had to be accommodated. When the minister reached the venue of the function, he was told that that the author of the book which he was to have released could not reach Mumbai as he was offloaded at Delhi.

The author was Professor Sengupta.

The British M.P., Beesie Braddock once shouted at Churchill during a dinner party: "Mr. Churchill, you are drunk!"

Not one to take an insult lying down, Churchill shouted back: "And madam, you are ugly." Adding in the same breath, "But in the morning, I shall be sober."

Another man with pretensions of being a poet, sent his work to a publisher and pompously demanded an immediate reply, adding that "I have other irons in the fire."

The rejection slip bore this reply: "Remove the irons and insert the poems."

Churchill and Shaw were always at daggers drawn, though in a friendly way. Shaw invited Churchill to the opening night of one of his plays, sending two tickets, "one for yourself and one for a friend—if you have any." Churchill could not attend but asked if he could have tickets for the second night performance, "if there is one."

This is from a college in the Chambal belt.
"What kind of writing pays the best?"
"A ransom note."

A cabinet minister in the room next to Churchill's was shouting into the phone. Annoyed, he asked an aide to tell the minister to lower his voice. The aide came back and told, "He is talking to Washington."

"Then ask him to use the phone," was Churchill's caustic comment.

What is a writer's cramp called?
A: *Authoritis*

Proud poet: My book of poems has been published recently.
Friend: Did you sell any?
Poet: Yes, my clothes, watch and the gold chain.

One young, aspiring author boasted, "I can live very well on what I write."
"Really," asked another in their creative writing class: "What do you write?"
"Begging letters to my father."

IX

The Queen's English

It is often not realized that punctuation is a very important part of good prose. It prompted Lynne Truss, who presented a popular series on punctuation on BBC Radio 4, to write a best-selling book on the subject titled *Eats, Shoots* and *Leaves*. The title is a little intriguing, but it is based on a joke published originally, I think, in *Reader's Digest* long back. The joke goes like this:

A panda walks into a café. He orders a sandwich, eats it, then draws a gun and fires two shots in the air.

"Why?" asks the confused waiter, as the panda makes towards the exit. The panda produces a badly punctuated wildlife manual and tosses it over his shoulder.

"I'm a panda," he says at the door. "Look it up."

The waiter turns to the relevant entry and, sure enough, finds an explanation.

"*Panda*. Large black-and-white bear-like animal, native to China. *Eats, shoots and leaves.*"

The English professor slipped his arm around the waist of the comely housemaid just as his wife entered the room. "Really, Gopal," she exclaimed, "I am surprised at you."

"To the contrary, my dear," he corrected, "It is we, who are surprised. You are astonished."

The school manager and the principal did not carry on well and tried to run each other down to the detriment of school discipline. One day, the manager wrote on a class blackboard:

"The manager says the principal is a fool."

The principal did not take it lying down. He just inserted commas in the sentence to read:

"The manager, says the principal, is a fool."

This is true—believe it or not. There was once a professor of... (no, I won't tell you) whose English sometimes went for a six. Some of his isms:

"I think my room is lighter than yours."

"You can sleep over my wife; I am taking the other berth." You know what he meant actually.

In West Bengal, teaching in English in the middle school was discontinued decades back and has been reintroduced only lately, and so the teachers are struggling with the new subject. The following conversation was overheard recently in a school:

"Who is the headmaster?"

"I *is* the headmaster."

"So, you are the headmaster."

"Yes, I *are* the headmaster."

A brash new lecturer in English was bragging about his power with words. He boasted he could reel out synonyms of any word.

A senior deflated his ego by asking: "Tell me another word for thesaurus."

Some school students in Bihar were vying over, who was most patriotic. Said one: "I never use imported goods." Another said: "I never see foreign movies." The third averred: "I have never passed English since I started school."

(The conversation, of course, was in Bhojpuri Hindi.)

These days, there is a rush to learn English. One *Bihari* boy memorized a few phrases from an etiquette book. When a cup of tea was handed to him at a party, he responded: "Thank you, sir or madam, as the case may be."

Recently, I had another encounter with malapropism. The principal of the women's college commiserating with a girl with a badly burnt face said, "Don't worry, dear, with *cosmic* surgery, the scars will disappear."

The class was given to write an essay on 'Comparing the joys of youth and old age'. A pupil wrote: "Great are the pleasures of youth, but nothing as compared to the pleasures of *adultery*."

The English teacher was in labour with her first child when she suddenly started shouting: "Can't, won't, don't, didn't, doesn't, couldn't, wouldn't, shouldn't. . . ."

Perplexed, the nurse asked: "Doctor, what's wrong with the patient?"

"Oh! she's having contractions," reassured the doctor.

Reverend William A. Spooner of New College, Oxford, had the habit of transposing the initial sounds of two or more words while speaking, often to humorous effect—from which was coined the word, *spoonerism*. On one occasion, he chided a student, "You have *hissed* my *mystery* lecture." And in disgust added: "You have *tasted* two *werms*." Another one from him: "It is *kisstomary* to *cuss* the bride."

Another girl wrote in her geography test:
"The climate is hottest at the *creator*."

No, this didn't happen in Bihar. It actually happened in Saugar University, Madhya Pradesh. On the first day of the session, a teacher took her English literature class and naturally lectured in English. Complained mournfully the class: "Hey, this Madam teaches English in English!"

The college garden was in full bloom in the winter, and the half-literate gardener boasted, "We have flowers of all colours of the *rectum*."

A yokel from Patna had a windfall inheritance and started to have social ambitions. He joined an etiquette course to learn social graces. When a neighbour died, he went to console the family. As taught by the etiquette advisor, he commiserated, "She was not only your mother but was so good that the whole neighbourhood considered her their mother." The teacher complemented him for being a good learner and he became very proud of his social accomplishments.

Later, the wife of a friend died. The man went to condole his friend. "I am very sorry to learn of your wife's death. She was not only your wife but was considered the wife of us all."

In an answer to a question on a sociology test, "Why did the population of Mumbai grow so rapidly?" A student wrote: "The population of Mumbai grew fast because of the large *stork yard.*"

When his daughter passed the high school examination in the first division, the neighbours came to felicitate her: "*Consolations* on your brilliant success."

The magistrate asked the witness: "Who is making the allegation?"
    A man stood up and said: "Sir, I am the *alligator.*"

A newspaper report:
    "*Adulterous* references were made to the scientist, who did a pioneering work on water harvesting in the Bikaner district."

A number of well-wishers, who called to condole the author Khushwant Singh when his mother died said they had come '*to condone*' his mother's death.

A news item:

The education minister has announced free education up to the *muddle* class.

A take on punctuation is provided by the actress, Katherine hepburn.

This is what she has to say: "I hate punctuating with full stops. They are so final like death. I use a dash instead of a full stop. And commas bother me. When I use one, I think I have stubbed my toes. However, I haven't made up my mind about question marks."

A kind of spoonerism is interposition of whole words. Such transposition of words is called *metathesis* and occurs not infrequently. "I am going to plant my water today."

"I need to put these eyes thrice in the drops daily."

Medigogy

These days many newly-passed medicos don't care to take the Hippocratic Oath. They now believe in *Hypocrites Oath*.

R.L. Stevenson probably had in mind some of the Indian medicos, who got admission on leaked question papers when he wrote, *The Strange Case of Dr. Jekyll and Mr. Hyde*. Such doctors kill and then hide!

The doctor from the All-India Institute of Medical Sciences called to treat the American ambassador who had this to tell His Excellency: "Sir, diplomatic immunity doesn't give you immunity from disease in India."

Professor Mathur of the Agra Medical College tells this story: "We were in Paris to attend a conference. We were served only wine at meals and desperately wanted a drink of water, but couldn't make the waiters understand because they didn't know English and we didn't know French. Desperate, we asked the hosts the word for water. 'Aqua,' he said. And all our lives, we have been writing 'aqua' for water in our prescriptions!"

The professor of medicine gave this practical advice in his valedictory address to the passing graduates:

"If you know not what the problem is and do not know how to cure it, call it an allergy."

The demonstrator of the medico-legal department was guiding the budding medicos. He said that if a man was brought for autopsy with slit throat and a bullet lodged in his chest, what would be the first thing that the student should look for?"

A bright student said, "I would first see whether there was any evidence of foul play."

There was a long queue at the pathology lab of the medical college. When the turn of the girl came after three hours, she turned to her mother and quipped: "I now know why a sick person is called a *patient*."

He was admitted in the medical college hospital with an injury. The student nurse came into the ward where he was lying and gave him an injection. The jab of the needle was so sharp that he roared with pain.

Worried, his wife wanted to know, "What was that?"

The nurse told her, "A pain-killer."

Soon after passing out of the military nursing school, the girl gushed to her family: "I have been allotted to the infantry—you know, I have always loved children."

During the final surgery examination, the professor asked a student, "Why do surgeons wear a mask during operations?"

"So if anything goes wrong," the student offered, "no one can recognize them."

Soon after Independence, a newly appointed health minister goes for inspection of the medical college. He brightens up in the department of radiology. "Well, I have a radio which is not working. I will send it along. Please set it right," he requests the professor. (Yes, I know it's an old one; but I will bring it anyway!)"

In some north Indian medical colleges, students went on strike at the drop of a hat grievously disrupting patient care. During one such flash strike, one disgusted patient decided, "Well, I think I will go home and die a natural death."

The doctor was examining the mother with a stethoscope. The three-year-old whispered to his older sister: "What is the doctor doing?"

"You silly, the doctor is telephoning mother's inside to find out what is wrong," was the all-knowing reply.

Asked by the examiner to describe the spinal column, a budding medico wrote: "The spinal column is a long string of bones: The head sits on the top, and you sit on the bottom."

At his anatomy practical, a student was required to draw and label a cross section of the spinal cord. After labelling the "Grey Matter" and the "White Matter" he was not sure what the remaining part was. He finally labelled it as "Doesn't Matter."

A fellow was getting frequent headaches and the doctor he consulted tried hard but could not help him. So he went to eminent professor of neurology, who asked: "Well now, who treated you before?"

"Dr. Raman."

"I see. He is an idiot. I would like to know what he advised you to do. The fellow: "That I should come and consult you."

The professor of urology died. The condolence resolution passed by the college said:

"May his soul rest in *piss*."

After giving a thorough check-up, the famous physician told the patient: "I can't find a cause for your complaint. Frankly, I think it is due to drinking."

"In that case," said the patient, "I'll come back when you are sober."

Deft definition of a thermometer: "The only thing that is graduated with degrees but without any brains."

www.ingramcontent.com/pod-product-compliance
Lightning Source LLC
Chambersburg PA
CBHW070337230426
43663CB00011B/2354